CHINESE LOVE STORIES

爱情故事

https://ChineseLoveStories.com/

VOLUME 2

YIRAN LU

陆依然

©2024 YIRAN LU. All rights reserved.

ACKNOWLEDGEMENT

Thank you everyone for inspiring me to write the books. I am deeply indebted to all of you. Thank you, dear almighty.

YIRAN LU

INTRODUCTION

Do you like reading short stories? How about the love stories? Well, learning a language like Mandarin Chinese can be long and time-consuming process. However, if you learn reading Chinese love stories, you'd be able to keep the language learning motivation high while appreciating the Chinese language and culture. In this book series, designed for the Chinese language students, you will learn reading Chinese short stories. Each book comes with about twenty romantic stories. The stories are provided in both English and Chinese. A list of selected keywords (English, pinyin, and Chinese) from the Chinese text if included for a quick reference. Taken together, these books are suitable for all levels (beginners to advanced HSK levels) of Mandarin Chinese students. Happy learning. :)

CONTENTS

ACKNOWLEDGEMENT 2

INTRODUCTION 3

CONTENTS 4

Chapter 1: Moonlit Vow 8
标题 8
故事 8
关键词 8
英文翻译 9

Chapter 2: A Blooming Romance 10
标题 10
故事 10
关键词 10
英文翻译 11

Chapter 3: A Romance Under the Moonlight with the Qin 13
标题 13
故事 13
关键词 14
英文翻译 14

Chapter 4: Moonlit Romance 16
标题 16
主要故事 16
关键词及其含义 16
英文翻译 17

Chapter 5: The Promise of the Red Silk 18
标题 18

主要故事 18

关键词及其含义 18

英文翻译 19

Chapter 6: The Red Thread of Fate 21

标题 21

主要故事 21

关键词及其含义 21

英文翻译 22

Chapter 7: Beneath the Moonlight Among the Flowers 24

标题 24

主要故事 24

关键词 24

英文翻译 25

Chapter 8: Harmony of Lute and Zither 26

标题 26

主要故事 26

关键词 27

英文翻译 27

Chapter 9: The Red Thread of Yuelao 29

标题 29

故事 29

关键词及含义 29

故事英文翻译 30

Chapter 10: The Vow Beneath the Cherry Blossoms 31

标题 31

故事 31

关键词及含义 31

故事英文翻译 32

Chapter 11: Beneath the Moon, in Front of the Flowers 33

    标题 33

    故事 33

    关键词 33

    英文翻译 34

Chapter 12: The Red Thread of Fate 36

    标题 36

    主要故事 36

    关键词及其含义 36

    英文翻译 37

Chapter 13: A Serendipitous Encounter in the Rainy South of the Yangtze River 38

    标题 38

    主要故事 38

    关键词及其含义 39

    英文翻译 39

Chapter 14: A Romance on the Bridge 41

    标题 41

    故事 41

    关键词 42

    英文翻译 42

Chapter 15: A Promise Under the Starlight 44

    标题 44

    主要故事 44

    关键词及其含义 45

    英文翻译 45

Chapter 16: Love Letters Through Time 47

    标题 47

    故事 47

关键词及含义 47

英文版故事 48

Chapter 17: The Vow Beneath the Starlight 49

标题 49

故事 49

关键词及含义 49

英文版故事 50

Chapter 18: Eternal Kiss 51

标题：永恒之吻 - Yǒng Héng Zhī Wěn - Eternal Kiss 51

故事： 51

关键词及英语含义： 51

英文版故事： 52

Chapter 19: A Heartwarming Romance Story 54

标题 54

故事 54

关键词及含义 54

英文版故事 55

Chapter 20: Love that Captivates a City 56

标题 56

故事 56

关键词及英语含义 56

英文版故事 57

Chapter 1: Moonlit Vow

标题

月下誓言（Yuè Xià Shì Yán）

Moonlit Vow

故事

在古老的中国，有一个名叫[李婉儿（Lǐ Wǎnr）]的美丽女子，她聪明伶俐，琴棋书画样样精通。在一个月色如水的夜晚，婉儿在花园中弹琴，琴音悠扬，仿佛能穿透夜空，触及星辰。

此时，一个名叫[张云轩（Zhāng Yún Xuān）]的青年书生路过，被琴声深深吸引。他驻足聆听，心中不禁涌起一股莫名的情感。云轩走近婉儿，两人四目相对，仿佛时间在这一刻停滞。

他们开始交谈，从诗词歌赋到人生哲学，彼此都感到异常投契。云轩被婉儿的才情和美貌深深打动，而婉儿也对云轩的才华和风度倾心不已。

月色愈发明亮，两人决定在月下立下誓言。云轩从怀中取出一块玉佩，上面刻着一只凤凰，象征着吉祥和幸福。他深情地望着婉儿，将玉佩轻轻递给她，说道："我愿与你共度此生，无论贫穷还是富有，无论疾病还是健康，都不离不弃。"

婉儿接过玉佩，眼中闪烁着泪光，她微笑着回应："我愿与你携手共度风雨，直到海枯石烂，永不变心。"

两人紧紧相拥，月光洒在他们身上，仿佛为他们披上了一层神圣的光辉。从此，他们过上了幸福的生活，共同书写了一段传世佳话。

关键词
- 李婉儿（Lǐ Wǎnr）: Li Waner (Beautiful woman named Li)
- 张云轩（Zhāng Yún Xuān）: Zhang Yunxuan (Talented scholar named Zhang)
- 月色（Yuè Sè）: Moonlight

- 誓言（Shì Yán）: Vow
- 玉佩（Yù Pèi）: Jade pendant

英文翻译

Moonlit Vow

In ancient China, there lived a beautiful woman named Li Waner. She was intelligent and skilled in various arts, including music, chess, calligraphy, and painting. On a moonlit night, Waner played her lute in the garden, and the melodious music seemed to pierce the night sky and touch the stars.

At that moment, a young scholar named Zhang Yunxuan passed by and was deeply attracted by the music. He stopped to listen, and a strange feeling welled up in his heart. Yunxuan approached Waner, and when their eyes met, it seemed as if time had stopped.

They began to talk, discussing poetry, songs, books, and the meaning of life. Yunxuan was deeply moved by Waner's talent and beauty, and Waner was also captivated by Yunxuan's wisdom and elegance.

As the moon grew brighter, they decided to make a vow under the moonlight. Yunxuan took out a jade pendant from his chest, with a phoenix carved on it, symbolizing good fortune and happiness. Gazing deeply into Waner's eyes, he gently handed her the pendant and said, "I vow to spend the rest of my life with you, through poverty and riches, sickness and health, never to part."

Waner took the pendant with tears in her eyes and smiled as she replied, "I vow to walk through life's storms with you, until the sea dries up and the rocks crumble, never to change my heart."

They hugged tightly, and the moonlight shone on them, as if it had draped them in a sacred glow. From then on, they lived a happy life together, leaving behind a legendary tale that would be passed down through the ages.

Chapter 2: A Blooming Romance

标题

缘起桃花（**Yuán Qǐ Táo Huā**）

A Blooming Romance

故事

在江南水乡，有个名叫[柳梦溪（Liǔ Mèng Xī）]的女子，她如同她的名字一样，温柔如梦，美丽如溪。每年春天，她家院中的桃树都会盛开满树的桃花，吸引无数游客驻足观赏。

有一天，一个来自京城的青年画家[赵逸飞（Zhào Yì Fēi）]途径此地，被柳梦溪家的桃花深深吸引。他停下脚步，拿出画笔，开始捕捉这美景。

柳梦溪好奇地走了过来，看到赵逸飞笔下的桃花栩栩如生，仿佛每一朵都在微风中轻轻摇曳。她被他的画技深深吸引，主动与他攀谈起来。

两人从桃花聊起，渐渐发现彼此有着许多共同的兴趣爱好。他们一起漫步在桃花林中，谈诗论画，笑语盈盈。赵逸飞被柳梦溪的才情和美貌所打动，而柳梦溪也对赵逸飞的才华和风度倾心不已。

桃花盛开的日子一天天过去，两人的感情也越发深厚。终于有一天，赵逸飞鼓起勇气，在满树桃花的见证下，向柳梦溪表白了他的爱意。

柳梦溪羞涩地低下头，轻声说道："我也愿意与你共度此生，在这桃花盛开的地方，让我们的爱情永远绽放。"

于是，两人在桃花树下许下了誓言，决定携手共度未来的日子。他们的爱情故事也成为了当地的一段佳话，流传至今。

关键词

- 柳梦溪（Liǔ Mèng Xī）: Liu Mengxi (A gentle and beautiful woman named Liu)
- 赵逸飞（Zhào Yì Fēi）: Zhao Yifei (A talented painter named Zhao)

- 桃花（Táo Huā）: Peach Blossom (A symbol of love and romance in Chinese culture)
- 誓言（Shì Yán）: Vow (A solemn promise)

英文翻译

A Blooming Romance

In the picturesque riverside town of Jiangnan, there lived a woman named Liu Mengxi. She was as gentle and beautiful as her name suggested, resembling a dreamy stream. Every spring, the peach tree in her courtyard would bloom with an abundance of flowers, attracting numerous visitors to admire its beauty.

One day, a young painter from the capital, Zhao Yifei, traveled through the town and was captivated by the peach blossoms in Liu Mengxi's courtyard. He stopped, took out his brush, and began to capture the scenic view.

Liu Mengxi, curious, walked over and saw Zhao Yifei's painting come to life as if each peach blossom was gently swaying in the breeze. Fascinated by his skill, she initiated a conversation with him.

The two struck up a conversation about the peach blossoms and soon discovered they shared many common interests. They walked through the peach orchard, discussing poetry and painting, their laughter and smiles echoing throughout the grove. Zhao Yifei was captivated by Liu Mengxi's talent and beauty, while Liu Mengxi was equally drawn to Zhao Yifei's artistic prowess and gentlemanly demeanor.

As the days of blooming peach blossoms passed, the two grew closer. Eventually, Zhao Yifei gathered his courage and confessed his love for Liu Mengxi under the watchful gaze of the blooming trees.

Liu Mengxi blushed and lowered her head, whispering, "I also wish to spend my life with you, amidst these blooming peach blossoms, letting our love flourish forever."

The two made a vow under the peach tree, deciding to embark on a journey of life together. Their romantic tale became a local legend, passed down through the generations.

Chapter 3: A Romance Under the Moonlight with the Qin

标题

月下琴缘（**Yuè Xià Qín Yuán**）

A Romance Under the Moonlight with the Qin

故事

在古老的江南水乡，有个名叫[苏婉儿（Sū Wǎn'ér）]的琴师，她的琴声悠扬，如流水般清澈。每到夜晚，她都会坐在月下的竹林中，弹奏她的古琴，那琴声能穿越竹林，飘向远方。

一天，一个名叫[陆云轩（Lù Yún Xuān）]的书生途径此地，被苏婉儿的琴声深深吸引。他循声而来，只见月光下，一位佳人正专注地弹奏着古琴。那琴声如诉如泣，仿佛在诉说着一个古老的故事。

陆云轩被那琴声深深打动，他站在竹林外，静静地聆听。直到琴声停止，他才鼓起勇气上前与苏婉儿交谈。两人一见如故，从诗词歌赋谈到琴棋书画，彼此都感到十分投缘。

此后，每到夜晚，陆云轩都会来到竹林，与苏婉儿共赏月色，聆听琴声。他们的感情在琴声和月光的见证下，越发深厚。然而，陆云轩因家中事务需要离开江南，两人不得不暂别。

临别之际，苏婉儿将她的古琴赠与陆云轩，并嘱咐他："愿君常记此琴声，常念此月色。"陆云轩含泪收下，承诺一定会回来找她。

几年后，陆云轩终于完成了家中事务，他带着古琴回到了江南。然而，当他来到竹林时，却发现苏婉儿已经离开，只留下一封书信和一块玉佩。书信中写道："琴声依旧，月色如初，但人已非昨。愿君安好，珍重。"

陆云轩痛失挚爱，他抱着古琴和玉佩，坐在月下，弹奏起那首熟悉的曲子。琴声悠扬，仿佛穿越了时空，与苏婉儿的琴声相互呼应。

关键词
- 苏婉儿（Sū Wǎn'ér）：Su Waner (A skilled female musician)
- 陆云轩（Lù Yún Xuān）：Lu Yunxuan (A scholarly young man)
- 古琴（Gǔ Qín）：Guqin (A traditional Chinese stringed instrument)
- 月下（Yuè Xià）：Under the Moonlight (A romantic setting)
- 琴缘（Qín Yuán）：Bond of Music (A connection formed through music)

英文翻译

A Romance Under the Moonlight with the Qin

In the ancient riverside town of Jiangnan, there lived a skilled musician named Su Waner. Her qin music was melodious, as clear as flowing water. Every night, she would sit in a bamboo forest under the moonlight, playing her guqin. The music would drift through the bamboo, carrying far into the distance.

One day, a scholarly young man named Lu Yunxuan traveled through the town and was deeply captivated by Su Waner's qin music. He followed the sound and found a beautiful woman playing the guqin under the moon. The music seemed to tell an ancient story, filled with emotion.

Lu Yunxuan was deeply moved by the music. He stood outside the bamboo forest, listening quietly. After the music stopped, he gathered his courage and approached Su Waner to strike up a conversation. The two hit it off immediately, discussing poetry, calligraphy, painting, and chess. They felt a strong connection with each other.

From then on, every night, Lu Yunxuan would come to the bamboo forest to admire the moonlight and listen to Su Waner's qin music. Their bond grew deeper under the witness of the qin music and the moonlight. However, Lu Yunxuan had to leave Jiangnan due to family matters, and the two had to part temporarily.

Before leaving, Su Waner gave her guqin to Lu Yunxuan and said, "Remember this music and this moonlit night always." Lu Yunxuan tearfully accepted the gift and promised to return.

Years later, Lu Yunxuan finally finished his family matters and returned to Jiangnan with the guqin. However, when he arrived at the bamboo forest, he found that Su Waner had left, leaving only a letter and a jade pendant. The letter said, "The music remains, the moon is still as bright, but people have changed. Wishing you well and take care."

Lu Yunxuan was devastated by the loss of his beloved. Holding the guqin and jade pendant, he sat under the moon and played the familiar tune. The melodious music seemed to transcend time and space, echoing with Su Waner's qin music.

Chapter 4: Moonlit Romance

标题

月下情缘 (Yuè Xià Qíng Yuán)

Moonlit Romance

主要故事

在古老的江南水乡，有一个名叫杨柳（Yáng Liǔ）的女子，她容貌秀丽，心地善良。杨柳每日在江边浣纱，她的歌声总能引来过路行人的驻足。而在江的对岸，住着一位名叫张生（Zhāng Shēng）的书生，他才华横溢，温文尔雅。

两人虽未曾谋面，但彼此的才情与美丽早已传遍了水乡。每当夜幕降临，明月高悬，张生便会站在江边，隔江凝望杨柳的身影，而杨柳也时常在歌声中流露出对张生的思念。

终于有一天，张生鼓起勇气，租了一叶扁舟，横渡江水，来到了杨柳的身旁。两人一见如故，仿佛多年的知己。他们一起在江边漫步，谈诗论道，欢声笑语不断。

随着时间的推移，两人的感情日益深厚。张生为了杨柳，放弃了京城的功名，决定留在水乡与她共度余生。而杨柳也为了张生，放弃了浣纱的生活，开始学习琴棋书画，陪伴在他的身边。

最终，两人喜结连理，过上了幸福美满的生活。他们的故事传遍了整个水乡，成为了人们津津乐道的佳话。每当夜幕降临，明月高悬，人们总会想起那对月下情缘的恋人，感叹爱情的伟大与美好。

关键词及其含义

- 杨柳 (Yáng Liǔ)：一个美丽的女子
- 张生 (Zhāng Shēng)：一个才华横溢的书生
- 江南水乡 (Jiāngnán Shuǐxiāng)：指中国南方的水乡地区，以优美的自然风光和丰富的文化底蕴著称
- 月下情缘 (Yuè Xià Qíng Yuán)：指发生在月光下的浪漫爱情

英文翻译

Moonlit Romance

In the ancient watery town of Jiangnan, there lived a woman named Yang Liu. She was beautiful and kind-hearted. Every day, Yang Liu washed her silk fabrics by the riverbank, and her singing voice would often draw the attention of passersby. On the other side of the river lived a scholar named Zhang Sheng, who was talented and refined.

Although they had never met, their talents and beauty had spread throughout the town. Whenever night fell and the moon hung high, Zhang Sheng would stand by the riverbank, gazing across the water at Yang Liu's figure. Similarly, Yang Liu often expressed her longing for Zhang Sheng through her songs.

One day, Zhang Sheng summoned his courage and rented a small boat to cross the river and approach Yang Liu. The two struck up an immediate bond, as if they had been friends for years. They walked together by the riverbank, discussing poetry and philosophy, laughing and talking merrily.

As time passed, their feelings grew deeper. Zhang Sheng gave up the chance for fame and fortune in the capital and decided to stay in the watery town with Yang Liu. In turn, Yang Liu abandoned her life of washing silk and began to learn music, chess, calligraphy, and painting to accompany Zhang Sheng.

Eventually, the two were married and led a happy and fulfilling life. Their story spread throughout the town, becoming a much-talked-about tale of romance. Whenever night fell and the moon hung high, people would remember the lovers of Moonlit Romance and marvel at the greatness and beauty of love.

Chapter 5: The Promise of the Red Silk

标题

红绸之约 (Hóng Chóu Zhī Yuē)
The Promise of the Red Silk

主要故事

在繁华的京城，有一位名叫苏婉儿（Sū Wǎn'ér）的绣娘，她的手艺精湛，尤其擅长绣制红绸。她的红绸作品色泽鲜艳，寓意吉祥，深受达官贵人的喜爱。然而，苏婉儿心中却有一个未了的心愿——找到能读懂她心中绣画的人。

一日，京城举办了一场盛大的诗会，吸引了无数文人墨客。苏婉儿也带着自己的红绸作品前来参加，希望能借此机会找到那个特别的人。在诗会上，她遇见了一位名叫李墨轩（Lǐ Mò Xuān）的才子。他的诗词清新脱俗，字里行间流露出对美好事物的向往。

李墨轩被苏婉儿的红绸作品深深吸引，他驻足欣赏，赞叹不已。他看出每一幅红绸作品都蕴含着独特的故事和情感。苏婉儿见李墨轩如此懂她，心中不禁涌起一股暖流。两人相谈甚欢，仿佛找到了彼此的灵魂伴侣。

随着时间的推移，李墨轩和苏婉儿的感情越发深厚。他们一同品诗作画，一同赏花赏月，度过了许多美好的时光。终于，在一个春光明媚的日子里，李墨轩向苏婉儿求婚，并承诺要用一生的时间守护她。

苏婉儿感动不已，她将自己最珍爱的一幅红绸作品作为信物送给了李墨轩。那幅作品上绣着两只相依相偎的鸳鸯，寓意着两人将永远相亲相爱、不离不弃。李墨轩接过红绸作品，紧紧抱住苏婉儿，两人许下了永恒的誓言。

从此，李墨轩和苏婉儿过上了幸福美满的生活。他们的爱情故事传遍了整个京城，成为了人们津津乐道的佳话。而那幅红绸作品也成为了他们爱情的见证，永远珍藏在他们的心中。

关键词及其含义
- 苏婉儿（Sū Wǎn'ér）：故事中的女主角，一位技艺高超的绣娘。

- 李墨轩（Lǐ Mò Xuān）：故事中的男主角，一位才华横溢的才子。
- 红绸（Hóng Chóu）：指苏婉儿擅长的绣品，也象征着吉祥和美好。
- 诗会（Shī Huì）：古代文人墨客聚集在一起吟诗作赋的盛会。
- 鸳鸯（Yuān Yāng）：中国传统文化中的象征性动物，常用来比喻夫妻恩爱、形影不离。

英文翻译

The Promise of the Red Silk

In the bustling capital city, there lived a skilled embroiderer named Su Waner. Her embroidery skills were exceptional, especially when it came to the art of red silk. Her red silk works were vibrant in color and laden with auspicious meanings, deeply favored by the nobility. However, Su Waner had an unfulfilled wish in her heart—to find someone who could truly understand the paintings embroidered in her heart.

One day, a grand poetry gathering was held in the capital, attracting numerous literati and poets. Su Waner brought her red silk works to the gathering, hoping to find that special someone. There, she encountered a talented scholar named Li Moxuan. His poems were fresh and original, revealing a yearning for beauty in every line.

Li Moxuan was deeply captivated by Su Waner's red silk works. He stood there admiring them, marveling at their beauty. He could see that each work contained a unique story and emotion. Su Waner felt a warm current flowing through her heart as she saw how much Li Moxuan understood her. The two spoke fondly with each other, as if they had found each other's soulmate.

As time passed, the bond between Li Moxuan and Su Waner grew deeper. They enjoyed poetry and painting together, appreciating flowers and the moon, spending countless blissful moments. Finally, on a bright spring day, Li Moxuan proposed marriage to Su Waner, promising to protect her for a lifetime.

Deeply moved, Su Waner gave Li Moxuan her most precious red silk work as a token of affection. The work depicted two mandarin ducks nestling together, symbolizing that the two of them would always be inseparable and deeply in love.

Li Moxuan took the red silk work, hugged Su Waner tightly, and the two made a promise of forever.

From then on, Li Moxuan and Su Waner lived a happy and fulfilling life. Their love story spread throughout the capital, becoming a much-talked-about tale of romance. And that red silk work became a testament to their love, forever cherished in their hearts.

Chapter 6: The Red Thread of Fate

标题

月老红线 (Yuè Lǎo Hóng Xiàn)
The Red Thread of Fate

主要故事

在古老的中国，流传着一个关于月老与红线的传说。月老是天上的神祇，掌管着人间的姻缘。他有一卷红线，能将有缘人的心紧紧相连。

在一个宁静的小镇上，住着两位年轻人，男子叫文轩（Wén Xuān），女子名雅琴（Yǎ Qín）。文轩是个才华横溢的书生，而雅琴则是镇上最美丽的女子，能歌善舞。两人虽彼此倾慕，却从未有机会相识。

一日，月老在巡视人间时，发现了文轩和雅琴的缘分。他微笑着取出一根红线，轻轻一挥，红线便缠绕在两人的手腕上。与此同时，镇上举办了一场盛大的庙会，文轩和雅琴不约而同地来到了庙会。

在熙熙攘攘的人群中，文轩和雅琴被红线牵引着，最终相遇了。他们四目相对，仿佛时间在这一刻静止。两人被对方的气质深深吸引，开始交谈起来。他们发现彼此有着许多共同的兴趣爱好，话题不断。

庙会结束后，文轩和雅琴约定在镇上的小桥上再次相见。自那以后，他们常常相约游玩，感情日益加深。终于，在一个花好月圆的夜晚，文轩鼓起勇气，向雅琴表达了爱意。雅琴羞涩地点点头，两人紧紧相拥在一起。

不久后，文轩和雅琴在镇上举行了盛大的婚礼。他们的爱情故事传遍了整个小镇，成为了人们口中的佳话。而月老的红线，也成为了他们爱情永恒的见证。

关键词及其含义
- 月老 (Yuè Lǎo)：传说中的神仙，掌管人间姻缘。
- 红线 (Hóng Xiàn)：月老用来连接有缘人的神奇红线。
- 文轩 (Wén Xuān)：才华横溢的书生，故事中的男主角。

- 雅琴 (Yǎ Qín)：美丽善舞的女子，故事中的女主角。
- 庙会 (Miào Huì)：中国传统的民间活动，通常在节日或宗教节日时举行。

英文翻译

The Red Thread of Fate

In ancient China, there is a legend about Yue Lao and the red thread. Yue Lao is a deity in heaven who oversees the marriages of mortals. He has a roll of red thread that can tightly connect the hearts of destined souls.

In a quiet town, there lived two young people, a scholarly young man named Wen Xuan and a beautiful woman named Ya Qin. Wen Xuan was a talented scholar, while Ya Qin was the most beautiful woman in the town, skilled in singing and dancing. Though they admired each other from afar, they had never had a chance to meet.

One day, while surveying the human world, Yue Lao discovered the fateful connection between Wen Xuan and Ya Qin. With a smile, he took out a red thread and waved it gently, wrapping it around the wrists of the two. Meanwhile, a grand temple fair was being held in the town, and Wen Xuan and Ya Qin both came to the fair unintentionally.

Amidst the bustling crowd, Wen Xuan and Ya Qin were guided by the red thread and eventually met. Their eyes met, and it seemed as if time had stood still. Deeply attracted by each other's aura, they began to talk. They discovered that they had many common interests and hobbies, and their conversation flowed effortlessly.

After the temple fair, Wen Xuan and Ya Qin agreed to meet again on the small bridge in the town. Since then, they often met to play and spend time together, and their feelings grew deeper. Finally, on a night when the flowers bloomed and the moon was full, Wen Xuan took courage and confessed his love to Ya Qin. Ya Qin nodded shyly, and the two embraced tightly.

Not long after, Wen Xuan and Ya Qin held a grand wedding in the town. Their love story spread throughout the town, becoming a much-talked-about tale of romance. And Yue Lao's red thread became an eternal witness to their love.

Chapter 7: Beneath the Moonlight Among the Flowers

标题

中文：**月下花前**

拼音：**Yuè Xià Huā Qián**

英语：**Beneath the Moonlight Among the Flowers**

主要故事

在古老的江南水乡，有一个美丽的传说。故事的主人公是一对年轻的恋人——书生李明（Lǐ Míng）和绣娘张秀儿（Zhāng Xiù'ér）。李明温文尔雅，才情横溢，张秀儿则是巧手绣娘，绣出的花鸟栩栩如生。

两人相识于一个春意盎然的夜晚，当时明月高悬，繁花似锦。李明在花前月下吟诗作画，张秀儿则在不远处的绣楼中，一针一线地绣着美丽的图案。他们的目光偶然交汇，彼此的心中都泛起了涟漪。

随着时间的推移，两人的感情日渐深厚。他们常常相约在月下花前，共赏美景，共话未来。然而，天有不测风云，张秀儿的家族突遭变故，她被迫离开水乡，前往遥远的京城。

李明心如刀绞，但他并没有放弃。他发誓要找到张秀儿，与她共度余生。他踏上了漫漫寻妻之路，历经千辛万苦，终于在京城的一间绣坊里找到了张秀儿。

两人重逢的那一刻，所有的艰辛和等待都化作了幸福的泪水。他们紧紧相拥，仿佛要把所有的思念都融入这个拥抱之中。从此，他们过上了幸福的生活，继续在花前月下编织着属于他们的浪漫故事。

关键词

1. 月下花前 (Yuè Xià Huā Qián) - Beneath the Moonlight Among the Flowers: 形容景色优美，适合谈情说爱的场所。

2. 江南水乡 (Jiāng Nán Shuǐ Xiāng) - Jiangnan Water Towns: 指中国江南地区的水乡风光，富有诗意和浪漫气息。

3. 书生 (Shū Shēng) - Scholar: 古代读书人，通常指有文化、有才华的男性。

4. 绣娘 (Xiù Niáng) - Embroiderer: 擅长刺绣的女性工匠。

5. 寻妻之路 (Xún Qī Zhī Lù) - Journey to Find One's Wife: 形容为寻找妻子而经历的艰辛旅程。

英文翻译

Beneath the Moonlight Among the Flowers

In the ancient water towns of Jiangnan, there is a beautiful legend. The protagonists of the story are a young couple - the scholar Li Ming and the embroiderer Zhang Xiuer. Li Ming is gentle and talented, while Zhang Xiuer is skilled in embroidery, creating vivid patterns of flowers and birds.

The two met on a spring evening when the moon was high and the flowers were in full bloom. Li Ming was reciting poems and painting under the moonlight and flowers, while Zhang Xiuer was embroidering beautiful patterns in a nearby embroidery pavilion. Their eyes met by chance, and their hearts were filled with ripples.

As time went by, their feelings grew deeper. They often met under the moonlight and flowers to enjoy the scenery and talk about the future. However, misfortune struck Zhang Xiuer's family, and she was forced to leave the water town and travel to the distant capital city.

Li Ming's heart was torn, but he did not give up. He vowed to find Zhang Xiuer and spend the rest of his life with her. He embarked on a long journey to search for his wife, enduring hardships and challenges. Finally, he found Zhang Xiuer in an embroidery workshop in the capital city.

The moment they reunited, all the hardships and waiting were transformed into tears of happiness. They hugged tightly, as if to 融入所有的思念 into this embrace. From then on, they lived a happy life, continuing to weave their romantic story beneath the moonlight among the flowers.

Chapter 8: Harmony of Lute and Zither

标题
中文：**琴瑟和鸣**

拼音：**Qín Sè Hé Míng**

英语：**Harmony of Lute and Zither**

主要故事

在繁华的京城，有一个名叫赵子轩（Zhào Zǐ Xuān）的年轻才子，他精通音律，尤其擅长弹奏古琴。他的琴声如流水般悦耳，总能让人沉醉其中。

一日，赵子轩在郊外的小溪边弹奏古琴，琴声吸引了路过的苏婉儿（Sū Wǎn'ér）。苏婉儿是京城有名的才女，擅长弹奏古筝。她被赵子轩的琴声所吸引，不由自主地驻足聆听。

两人因音乐而相识，交谈甚欢。他们发现彼此对音乐都有着深厚的热爱和独特的见解。于是，他们开始一同合奏，赵子轩的古琴与苏婉儿的古筝相互呼应，琴声悠扬，和谐动听。

随着时间的推移，两人的感情越发深厚。他们一同游历名山大川，共同创作乐曲，分享彼此的生活点滴。然而，命运却给他们带来了考验。苏婉儿的家族因故需要她前往边疆，两人即将面临分别。

在分别之际，赵子轩为苏婉儿弹奏了一曲《离别》，琴声哀而不伤，充满了对未来的期待和祝福。苏婉儿泪眼婆娑，但她知道这是为了家族的责任。她紧紧握住赵子轩的手，承诺一定会回来。

几年后，苏婉儿履行了承诺，回到了京城。当她再次听到赵子轩的琴声时，两人相视而笑，所有的等待和思念都化作了幸福的泪水。他们再次合奏，琴声依旧悠扬，但更多了几分深沉和坚定。从此，他们过上了琴瑟和鸣、白头偕老的生活。

关键词

1. 琴瑟和鸣 (Qín Sè Hé Míng) - Harmony of Lute and Zither: 形容夫妻或恋人之间关系和谐，感情深厚。

2. 古琴 (Gǔ Qín) - Ancient Zither: 中国古代的一种弹拨乐器，音色优美。

3. 古筝 (Gǔ Zhēng) - Ancient Zither with Movable Bridges: 中国古代的一种弹拨乐器，音色明亮。

4. 离别 (Lí Bié) - Departure: 指离别、分别，常用于表达依依不舍的情感。

5. 白头偕老 (Bái Tóu Xié Lǎo) - Live Together Till Old Age: 形容夫妻恩爱，共度一生。

英文翻译

Harmony of Lute and Zither

In the bustling capital city, there lived a young talent named Zhao Zixuan, who excelled in music, especially in playing the ancient zither. His melodies flowed like a stream, captivating anyone who listened.

One day, Zhao Zixuan was playing his zither by a stream outside the city, and his music drew the attention of a passerby, Su Waner. Su Waner was a renowned talent in the capital, skilled in playing the guzheng. Drawn in by Zhao Zixuan's melodies, she stopped to listen intently.

The two met through music and struck up a lively conversation. They discovered that they both had a profound love for music and unique insights. Thus, they began to play together, Zhao Zixuan's zither and Su Waner's guzheng echoing each other, producing harmonious and enchanting melodies.

As time passed, their feelings grew deeper. They traveled together to visit famous mountains and rivers, composed music together, and shared the details of their daily lives. However, fate tested them with a challenge. Su Waner's family needed her to go to the border, and the two were soon to part.

Before their separation, Zhao Zixuan played a song titled "Farewell" for Su Waner. The melody was mournful yet hopeful, filled with anticipation and blessings for the future. Tears streamed down Su Waner's face, but she knew it was her responsibility to her family. She held Zhao Zixuan's hand tightly and promised to return.

After several years, Su Waner kept her promise and returned to the capital city. When she heard Zhao Zixuan's zither once again, they looked at each other and smiled. All the waiting and longing melted into tears of happiness. They played together again, and the melodies were still harmonious but with more depth and determination. From then on, they lived a life of harmony, sharing joys and sorrows until the end of their days.

Chapter 9: The Red Thread of Yuelao

标题

月老的红线

Yuè Lǎo De Hóng Xiàn

The Red Thread of Yuelao

故事

在一个古老的中国村庄里，住着一个年轻的书生，名叫子轩（Zǐ Xuān）。他聪明好学，却总是在情感上感到迷茫。村里的老人们常说，每个人的命运都由月老手中的红线牵引，子轩对此半信半疑。

一天，子轩在书店偶然遇到了一位名叫嫣然（Yān Rán）的美丽女子。两人一见如故，谈笑风生。子轩心中萌生了爱意，但他不知道嫣然是否也有同样的感觉。

不久，村里举行了一场盛大的庙会。在熙熙攘攘的人群中，子轩和嫣然意外地同时触摸到了一根悬挂在树上的红线。红线仿佛有灵性一般，紧紧缠绕在两人的手腕上，怎么也解不开。

村民们纷纷围观，有人说这是月老在牵线搭桥，让有情人终成眷属。子轩和嫣然相视一笑，心中都明白了彼此的心意。

从那天起，两人开始频繁地约会，共同欣赏诗词歌赋，漫步在月光下的田野间。他们的感情日益加深，红线也越发显得鲜艳夺目。

最终，在一个月圆之夜，子轩鼓起勇气向嫣然求婚。嫣然含羞地点头答应，两人紧紧相拥在一起。村民们纷纷祝福这对有情人，称赞月老的红线果然神奇。

关键词及含义
- 月老（Yuè Lǎo）：Moon Elder，传说中的神祇，负责掌管人间的姻缘。
- 红线（Hóng Xiàn）：Red Thread，象征着命中注定的缘分。

- 子轩（Zǐ Xuān）：Zi Xuan，男主角的名字。
- 嫣然（Yān Rán）：Yan Ran，女主角的名字。
- 庙会（Miào Huì）：Temple Fair，一种民间传统节日活动。

故事英文翻译

In an ancient Chinese village, there lived a young scholar named Zixuan. He was intelligent and studious, but always felt lost in matters of the heart. The elders in the village often spoke of the red thread held by Yuelao, the Moon Elder, who was said to be in charge of romantic destinies. Zixuan was skeptical but curious.

One day, Zixuan chanced upon a beautiful woman named Yanran in a bookstore. They hit it off immediately, sharing stories and laughter. Zixuan's heart fluttered with affection, but he didn't know if Yanran felt the same way.

Soon, the village held a grand temple fair. Amongst the bustling crowds, Zixuan and Yanran unexpectedly touched a red thread hanging from a tree. The thread seemed to come alive, wrapping tightly around their wrists, refusing to be undone.

Villagers gathered around, some saying that this was Yuelao's way of bringing lovers together. Zixuan and Yanran looked at each other with a smile, understanding each other's feelings.

From that day on, they met frequently, appreciating poetry and wandering through the moonlit fields. Their bond grew stronger, and the red thread glowed brighter.

Finally, on a night when the moon was full, Zixuan took the courage to propose to Yanran. She nodded shyly, and they embraced tightly. The villagers wished them well, marveling at the magic of Yuelao's red thread.

Chapter 10: The Vow Beneath the Cherry Blossoms

标题
樱花下的誓言

Yīng Huā Xià De Shì Yán

The Vow Beneath the Cherry Blossoms

故事

在春日的京都，有一片盛开的樱花林。每年的这个时候，无数恋人们都会来到这里，在漫天飞舞的樱花下许下爱的誓言。

林浩（Lín Hào）是一个年轻的音乐家，他来到京都寻找灵感。在樱花林中，他邂逅了一位美丽的女子，名叫晓雅（Xiǎo Yǎ）。她身着和服，宛如画中走出的仙子，手中捧着一本关于樱花的诗集。

两人被樱花的美丽所吸引，开始交谈。他们发现彼此都对音乐和诗歌有着浓厚的兴趣。林浩为晓雅弹奏了一曲自己创作的歌曲，晓雅则朗诵了一首赞美樱花的诗。在彼此的陪伴下，他们仿佛置身于一个只属于两人的浪漫世界。

随着时间的推移，两人越发相爱。他们一同漫步在樱花林中，一同欣赏月夜的樱花，一同度过了一个又一个美好的时光。在樱花即将凋零之际，林浩决定向晓雅求婚。

在樱花树下，林浩单膝跪地，手捧着一枚戒指，深情地看着晓雅。他发誓要永远守护她，与她共度余生。晓雅感动得泪流满面，她微笑着接受了林浩的求婚。

两人紧紧相拥在樱花树下，许下了永恒的誓言。那一刻，樱花瓣纷纷飘落，仿佛在为他们的爱情送上最真挚的祝福。

关键词及含义
- 樱花（Yīng Huā）：Cherry Blossom，代表浪漫和美丽。
- 京都（Jīng Dū）：Kyoto，日本古都，以樱花著名。

- 林浩（Lín Hào）：Lin Hao，男主角的名字。
- 晓雅（Xiǎo Yǎ）：Xiao Ya，女主角的名字。
- 誓言（Shì Yán）：Vow，两人许下的承诺。

故事英文翻译

In the springtime of Kyoto, there stands a cherry blossom forest in full bloom. Every year at this time, countless lovers gather here to make vows of love beneath the fluttering petals.

Lin Hao, a young musician, came to Kyoto to seek inspiration. In the cherry blossom forest, he encountered a beautiful woman named Xiao Ya. She wore a kimono, looking like a fairy stepping out of a painting, holding a book of poems about cherry blossoms.

Drawn by the beauty of the blossoms, they struck up a conversation. They discovered a shared passion for music and poetry. Lin Hao played a song he composed for Xiao Ya, while she recited a poem praising the cherry blossoms. Together, they seemed to be in a romantic world exclusive to them.

As time passed, their love grew deeper. They walked through the cherry blossom forest, admired the blossoms under the moonlit sky, and spent countless wonderful moments together. As the cherry blossoms were about to fade, Lin Hao decided to propose to Xiao Ya.

Beneath a cherry tree, Lin Hao knelt on one knee, holding a ring in his hand, looking deeply into Xiao Ya's eyes. He swore to protect her forever and spend the rest of his life with her. Xiao Ya was moved to tears, smiling as she accepted Lin Hao's proposal.

The two embraced tightly beneath the cherry tree, making a vow that would last forever. At that moment, cherry petals fell gracefully, as if offering the most sincere blessing for their love.

Chapter 11: Beneath the Moon, in Front of the Flowers

标题

月下花前：Yuè Xià Huā Qián

Beneath the Moon, in Front of the Flowers

故事

在古老的江南水乡，有一位才情横溢的书生，名叫李煜（Lǐ Yù）。他酷爱诗词，尤其喜欢在月色朦胧的夜晚，漫步于庭院中，欣赏那盛开的花朵。

一日，李煜在月下花前偶遇了一位名叫婉儿（Wǎn Ér）的美丽女子。她身穿淡雅的汉服，手中捧着一本诗集，眼中闪烁着对知识的渴望和对美好生活的向往。两人一见如故，相谈甚欢。

此后，李煜和婉儿常常相约在月下花前，共同品味诗词之美，分享彼此的喜怒哀乐。他们的感情日渐深厚，如同这盛开的花朵，在月光的照耀下越发绚烂。

然而，好景不长。李煜的父亲因官场纷争被迫离开了水乡，李煜也随之离去。两人被迫分离，心中充满了无尽的思念与哀伤。

在远方的日子里，李煜每日夜不能寐，思念着婉儿。他写下了无数诗篇，寄托着对婉儿的深情厚意。而婉儿也在水乡中，默默等待着李煜的归来。

终于，在一个月色如水的夜晚，李煜回到了水乡。他飞奔到婉儿的庭院，只见那盛开的花朵依旧娇艳，而婉儿也依旧美丽动人。两人紧紧相拥，泪水滑落在彼此的脸庞。

从此，李煜和婉儿在月下花前过上了幸福的生活。他们共同品味着诗词之美，享受着生活的甜蜜。他们的故事也成为了水乡中一段美丽的传说。

关键词
- 月下花前 (Yuè Xià Huā Qián) - Beneath the Moon, in Front of the Flowers
- 李煜 (Lǐ Yù) - Li Yu (a scholarly young man)

- 婉儿 (Wǎn Ér) - Wan'er (a beautiful young woman)
- 江南水乡 (Jiāng Nán Shuǐ Xiāng) - Jiangnan Water Town (a region in China famous for its waterways and beautiful scenery)
- 诗词 (Shī Cí) - Poetry (traditional Chinese poetry)
- 汉服 (Hàn Fú) - Han Clothing (traditional Chinese clothing)

英文翻译

Beneath the Moon, in Front of the Flowers

In the ancient Jiangnan Water Town, there lived a scholarly young man named Li Yu. He was passionate about poetry and especially enjoyed wandering in his courtyard, admiring the blooming flowers under the dim moonlight.

One day, Li Yu encountered a beautiful woman named Wan'er beneath the moon, in front of the flowers. She wore elegant Han Clothing and held a book of poetry in her hands, her eyes sparkling with a desire for knowledge and a longing for a better life. The two hit it off immediately and spoke heartily with each other.

After that, Li Yu and Wan'er often met beneath the moon, in front of the flowers, to appreciate the beauty of poetry and share their joys and sorrows. Their feelings grew deeper, like the blooming flowers, shining even more brilliantly under the moonlight.

However, good times didn't last long. Li Yu's father was forced to leave the water town due to political turmoil, and Li Yu followed him. The two were separated, filled with endless longing and sorrow.

In the distant days, Li Yu couldn't sleep at night, missing Wan'er deeply. He wrote countless poems, expressing his profound feelings for Wan'er. And Wan'er, in the water town, silently waited for Li Yu's return.

Finally, on a moonlit night, Li Yu returned to the water town. He ran to Wan'er's courtyard and saw that the blooming flowers were still gorgeous, and Wan'er was still beautiful and charming. The two hugged tightly, tears streaming down their faces.

From then on, Li Yu and Wan'er lived a happy life beneath the moon, in front of the flowers. They enjoyed the beauty of poetry together and savored the sweetness of life. Their story became a beautiful legend in the water town.

Chapter 12: The Red Thread of Fate

标题
中文：月老的红线
Pinyin：Yuè Lǎo de Hóng Xiàn
English：The Red Thread of Fate

主要故事
在古老的中国，有一位名叫月老的智者，他掌管着世间所有男女的姻缘。月老的手中有一卷红线，每一根红线都连接着两个命中注定的人。

有一日，京城的书生李明，在庙会上偶遇了卖花女小红。他们的目光交汇，仿佛时间在这一刻停滞。月老看到了这一幕，轻轻一笑，从红线卷中抽出一根，悄无声息地系在了李明和小红的脚踝上。

李明与小红相识后，发现彼此兴趣爱好惊人地相似，仿佛有说不完的话题。然而，他们的身份地位悬殊，李明的父母反对他与一个卖花女在一起。李明心中苦闷，不知所措。

就在这时，月老现身了。他告诉李明，真正的爱情不受身份地位的限制，只要两人心意相通，红线便会指引他们走向幸福。李明听后茅塞顿开，决定勇敢追求小红。

经过一番努力，李明终于说服了父母，与小红喜结连理。他们的婚礼上，月老再次出现，送上了最真挚的祝福。从此，李明和小红过上了幸福美满的生活。

关键词及其含义
- 月老（Yuè Lǎo）：The Moon Elder，传说中掌管姻缘的神仙。
- 红线（Hóng Xiàn）：The Red Thread，象征着命中注定的缘分。
- 命中注定（Mìng Zhōng Zhù Dìng）：Destined by fate，指命运安排好的事情。
- 姻缘（Yīn Yuán）：Marriage fate，指婚姻的缘分。

英文翻译

In ancient China, there was a wise man named Yue Lao, who was in charge of the marital fate of all men and women in the world. In his hands, there was a scroll of red threads, and each thread connected two destined people.

One day, a scholar named Li Ming encountered a flower girl named Xiaohong at a temple fair. Their eyes met, and it seemed as if time had stopped for a moment. Yue Lao saw this scene, smiled gently, and silently tied a red thread from the scroll around the ankles of Li Ming and Xiaohong.

After meeting, Li Ming and Xiaohong discovered that they had incredibly similar interests and hobbies, as if they had endless topics to discuss. However, their social status was vastly different, and Li Ming's parents opposed his relationship with a flower girl. Li Ming was perplexed and did not know what to do.

At this moment, Yue Lao appeared. He told Li Ming that true love was not limited by social status, and as long as two people's hearts were connected, the red thread would guide them to happiness. After hearing this, Li Ming suddenly understood and decided to bravely pursue Xiaohong.

After much effort, Li Ming finally convinced his parents and married Xiaohong. At their wedding, Yue Lao appeared again and offered them his sincerest blessings. From then on, Li Ming and Xiaohong lived a happy and fulfilling life.

Chapter 13: A Serendipitous Encounter in the Rainy South of the Yangtze River

标题

中文：烟雨江南的邂逅

Pinyin：Yān Yǔ Jiāng Nán de Xiè Hòu

English：A Serendipitous Encounter in the Rainy South of the Yangtze River

主要故事

在烟雨朦胧的江南水乡，有一个叫做杨柳的小镇。春天到来时，杨柳依依，水波粼粼，美不胜收。小镇上有个名叫林风的青年，他热爱诗词，常常在湖边吟诗作画。

一日，春雨绵绵，林风撑着一把油纸伞，漫步在湖边。突然，他听到一阵清脆的歌声，循声望去，只见一位身着粉色衣裙的女子正在雨中翩翩起舞，仿佛与雨融为一体。这女子名叫晴儿，她来自邻镇，也是一位热爱诗词的才女。

林风被晴儿的舞姿和歌声所吸引，忍不住上前与她交谈。两人一见如故，相谈甚欢。晴儿告诉林风，她曾在梦中见到过这个小镇和湖边的美景，没想到现实中真的存在。林风听后，心中一动，邀请晴儿一同在湖边作画，记录这美好的瞬间。

在画画的过程中，两人的心越靠越近。他们一起欣赏湖边的美景，一起讨论诗词歌赋，一起分享彼此的故事。渐渐地，他们发现彼此的灵魂是如此契合，仿佛早已相识多年。

然而，好景不长。晴儿因为家中变故，不得不离开小镇。在临别的那天，林风将一幅他们共同完成的画作送给晴儿，画中是烟雨朦胧的江南水乡和他们在湖边作画的情景。晴儿含泪收下画作，承诺一定会珍藏这份美好的回忆。

多年后，林风依然独自在湖边作画，心中却始终忘不了那个雨中的邂逅。而晴儿也在远方默默思念着这个曾经给予她温暖和美好的地方。

关键词及其含义

- 烟雨江南（Yān Yǔ Jiāng Nán）：The misty south of the Yangtze River，形容江南地区春天烟雨朦胧的美景。
- 邂逅（Xiè Hòu）：A chance encounter，意外的相遇或偶然相逢。
- 林风（Lín Fēng）：Lin Feng，故事中的男主角，热爱诗词的青年。
- 晴儿（Qíng Ér）：Qing'er，故事中的女主角，热爱诗词的邻镇才女。
- 油纸伞（Yóu Zhǐ Sǎn）：An oil-paper umbrella，中国传统雨具，具有浓厚的文化气息。

英文翻译

In the misty waterside town of Yangliu in the south of the Yangtze River, there lived a young man named Lin Feng. He had a passion for poetry and painting, often wandering by the lake with his brush and ink.

One spring day, when the rain was gentle and persistent, Lin Feng walked along the lakeside with an oil-paper umbrella. Suddenly, he heard a crisp singing voice and looked up to see a woman dressed in a pink dress dancing gracefully in the rain, as if she had merged with the rain itself. Her name was Qing'er, a talented woman from a neighboring town who also loved poetry.

Lin Feng was drawn to Qing'er's dance and voice, and he couldn't resist approaching her for a conversation. They struck up an instant friendship and talked animatedly. Qing'er told Lin Feng that she had once dreamed of this town and the beautiful scenery by the lake, not realizing it existed in reality. Upon hearing this, Lin Feng invited Qing'er to paint with him by the lakeside, capturing the moment's beauty.

As they painted together, their hearts drew closer. They admired the scenery, discussed poetry and songs, and shared their stories. Gradually, they realized their souls were so compatible, as if they had known each other for many years.

However, good times don't last forever. Due to a family emergency, Qing'er had to leave the town. On the day of her departure, Lin Feng gave Qing'er a painting they had completed together, depicting the misty south of the Yangtze River and their moment by the lakeside. Qing'er tearfully accepted the painting, promising to cherish the memory.

Years later, Lin Feng still painted alone by the lakeside, but his heart remained with the chance encounter in the rain. And in the distance, Qing'er also missed the place that had once given her warmth and beauty.

Chapter 14: A Romance on the Bridge

标题

缘起桥上：Yuán Qǐ Qiáo Shàng

A Romance on the Bridge

故事

在古老的苏州城，有一条名为"醉美"的河流，河上横跨着一座古老的桥，名叫"缘起桥"。传说，在这座桥上相遇的情侣，都会得到月老的祝福，他们的爱情将永恒不渝。

有一天，年轻的书生陆云（Lù Yún）来到苏州城游玩，他漫步在醉美河畔，偶然间走到了缘起桥上。此时，桥的另一端，一位名叫柳烟（Liǔ Yān）的绣娘正低头绣花，她的美丽与温柔吸引了陆云的注意。

两人目光交汇，仿佛有了一种奇妙的默契。陆云鼓起勇气，走上前去与柳烟交谈。他们聊起了诗词歌赋，聊起了生活中的点滴，彼此之间的心灵逐渐靠近。

从那以后，陆云和柳烟经常相约在缘起桥上见面。他们一同欣赏河畔的风景，一同品尝苏州的美食，一同度过了一个个甜蜜的时光。在月光的照耀下，他们的爱情像那河水一样，静静流淌，愈发深沉。

然而，命运却对他们开了一个玩笑。陆云的父亲突然病重，需要他回家继承家业。陆云面临着一个艰难的抉择：是留下与柳烟共度余生，还是回到家乡尽孝？

在内心的挣扎与纠结中，陆云决定回到家乡。他向柳烟告别，承诺会尽快回来找她。柳烟虽然不舍，但也理解陆云的苦衷，她含泪送别了陆云。

时光荏苒，几年后，陆云终于处理好了家中的事务。他迫不及待地回到了苏州城，回到了那座充满回忆的缘起桥上。当他再次站在桥上时，他惊喜地发现，柳烟依然在桥的另一端等待着他。

两人紧紧相拥，所有的等待与思念都在这一刻得到了释放。他们决定放下所有的顾虑，携手共度余生。从此，缘起桥上又多了一段美丽的传说。

关键词

- 缘起桥（Yuán Qǐ Qiáo）- Bridge of Destiny (a bridge where lovers meet and obtain the blessing of the god of marriage)
- 苏州城（Sū Zhōu Chéng）- Suzhou City (a city in China famous for its ancient gardens and canals)
- 醉美河（Zuì Měi Hé）- Drunkenly Beautiful River (a fictional river in the story)
- 陆云（Lù Yún）- Lu Yun (the male protagonist, a young scholar)
- 柳烟（Liǔ Yān）- Liu Yan (the female protagonist, a skilled embroiderer)
- 月老（Yuè Lǎo）- The God of Marriage (a deity who oversees marriages in Chinese mythology)

英文翻译

A Romance on the Bridge

In the ancient city of Suzhou, there was a river called "Drunkenly Beautiful" with an ancient bridge spanning it, named "Bridge of Destiny." It was said that couples who met on this bridge would receive the blessing of the God of Marriage, and their love would last forever.

One day, a young scholar named Lu Yun came to Suzhou for a visit. He walked along the Drunkenly Beautiful River and stumbled upon the Bridge of Destiny. On the other side of the bridge, a skilled embroiderer named Liu Yan was busy with her stitching, her beauty and gentleness catching Lu Yun's attention.

Their eyes met, and a strange sense of understanding passed between them. Lu Yun gathered his courage and approached Liu Yan to strike up a conversation. They talked about poetry, songs, and the small details of life, gradually drawing closer in spirit.

From then on, Lu Yun and Liu Yan often met on the Bridge of Destiny. They admired the scenery by the river, tasted the delicious food of Suzhou, and spent countless sweet moments together. Under the moonlight, their love flowed like the river, deepening with each passing day.

However, fate played a cruel trick on them. Lu Yun's father suddenly fell ill, and he was needed back home to inherit the family business. Lu Yun faced a difficult choice: stay with Liu Yan and spend the rest of his life with her, or return home to fulfill his filial duty.

After much inner struggle, Lu Yun decided to return home. He bid farewell to Liu Yan, promising to come back for her as soon as possible. Though reluctant, Liu Yan understood Lu Yun's predicament and tearfully saw him off.

Years passed, and after settling his family affairs, Lu Yun returned to Suzhou, eager to reunite with Liu Yan on the Bridge of Destiny. When he stood on the bridge again, he was 惊喜地发现（surprised to find） Liu Yan still waiting for him on the other side.

Chapter 15: A Promise Under the Starlight
标题
中文：星光下的誓言
Pinyin：Xīng Guāng Xià de Shì Yán
English：A Promise Under the Starlight

主要故事

在遥远的海边小镇，有一个名叫李阳的青年，他热爱摄影，尤其是夜晚的星空。而在这个小镇的另一头，住着一个名叫苏婉的女孩，她梦想着成为一名舞蹈家，用舞蹈诠释生命的美好。

一天晚上，李阳在海边拍摄星空时，意外地发现了正在海边独自跳舞的苏婉。她的舞姿轻盈而优雅，仿佛与星空融为一体。李阳被苏婉的舞蹈深深吸引，他忍不住拿起相机，记录下了这美好的瞬间。

拍摄结束后，李阳走上前去与苏婉交谈。两人聊得很投机，发现彼此都有着共同的梦想和追求。李阳向苏婉展示了他拍摄的星空照片，而苏婉则即兴为李阳跳了一段舞蹈。

在接下来的日子里，李阳和苏婉经常相约在海边，李阳拍摄星空，苏婉则在星空下跳舞。他们的感情在星光下悄然升温，彼此成为了对方生命中不可或缺的一部分。

然而，有一天，苏婉收到了一封来自大城市的舞蹈学院的录取通知书。她既兴奋又矛盾，因为她不想错过这个难得的机会，但又舍不得离开李阳和这片星空。

李阳知道后，鼓励苏婉去追求自己的梦想。他告诉苏婉，无论她走到哪里，他们的心都会紧紧相连。在苏婉离开前的那个晚上，两人在海边许下了一个誓言：无论未来如何变迁，他们都会永远相爱，直到地老天荒。

苏婉带着李阳的祝福和誓言，踏上了前往大城市的列车。而李阳则继续留在海边，用相机记录下每一片星空，期待着与苏婉再次相聚的那一天。

关键词及其含义

- 星光下的誓言（Xīng Guāng Xià de Shì Yán）：A Promise Under the Starlight，在星空下许下的承诺。
- 李阳（Lǐ Yáng）：Li Yang，故事中的男主角，热爱摄影的青年。
- 苏婉（Sū Wǎn）：Su Wan，故事中的女主角，梦想成为舞蹈家的女孩。
- 星空（Xīng Kōng）：Starry Sky，指夜晚的天空，星星闪烁的景象。
- 舞蹈学院（Wǔ Dǎo Xué Yuàn）：Dance Academy，专门培训舞蹈人才的高等教育机构。

英文翻译

In a remote seaside town, there lived a young man named Li Yang who had a passion for photography, especially the starry sky at night. On the other side of the town lived a girl named Su Wan, who dreamed of becoming a dancer, interpreting the beauty of life through dance.

One evening, while photographing the starry sky by the sea, Li Yang stumbled upon Su Wan dancing alone by the beach. Her graceful dance seemed to merge with the stars. Fascinated, Li Yang couldn't resist picking up his camera to capture this beautiful moment.

After the shoot, Li Yang approached Su Wan to strike up a conversation. They chatted amicably and discovered they had common dreams and aspirations. Li Yang showed Su Wan his photos of the starry sky, while Su Wan performed a dance spontaneously for him.

In the following days, Li Yang and Su Wan often met by the sea. Li Yang photographed the starry sky while Su Wan danced under it. Their feelings grew under the starlight, and they became indispensable to each other's lives.

However, one day, Su Wan received a letter of admission from a dance academy in a big city. She was both excited and conflicted, as she didn't want to miss this rare opportunity but was reluctant to leave Li Yang and the starry sky behind.

Upon learning of this, Li Yang encouraged Su Wan to pursue her dream. He told her that no matter where she went, their hearts would remain connected. On the night before Su Wan's departure, the two made a promise by the sea: no matter how the future unfolded, they would always love each other until the end of time.

With Li Yang's blessing and promise, Su Wan boarded the train to the big city. While Li Yang remained by the sea, capturing every starry sky with his camera, eagerly anticipating the day they would reunite.

Chapter 16: Love Letters Through Time

标题

岁月情书 (Suì Yuè Qíng Shū) - Love Letters Through Time

故事

在古老的小镇边缘，有一棵见证了无数春秋的梧桐树(wú tóng shù)，树下藏着一段跨越岁月的爱情故事。李明(Lǐ Míng)与苏婉(Sū Wǎn)，自幼便是邻家玩伴，青梅竹马，两小无猜。岁月如梭，他们一同走过了春的繁花、夏的热烈、秋的硕果与冬的静谧。

每年初雪飘落之时，李明都会悄悄在梧桐树下埋下一封手写的情书，记录下对苏婉日益深厚的情感。这些情书，如同时间的信使，静静地等待着被发现的那一刻。而苏婉，虽不明了李明的心意，却总能在不经意间感受到那份温暖与陪伴，心中也悄悄种下了情愫的种子。

转眼间，十年已过，两人都已长大成人，各自忙碌于生活的洪流中，偶尔的相遇也显得匆忙而短暂。直到一个冬日的午后，苏婉偶然间在整理旧物时，发现了那些被岁月尘封的情书。一封封拆开，字里行间流露出的深情与温柔，让她泪流满面。原来，她一直寻找的答案，就藏在这份默默无言的守护之中。

她决定，这个冬天，她要亲自写下回信，不仅是对过去的回应，更是对未来共同生活的期许。当李明再次来到梧桐树下，意外地发现了苏婉留下的信件，心中涌动的情感难以言表。两人终于在那棵见证了他们成长的梧桐树下，紧紧相拥，许下了相守一生的誓言。

关键词及含义

- 梧桐树 (wú tóng shù) - Wutong Tree：象征坚贞不渝的爱情。
- 青梅竹马 (qīng méi zhú mǎ) - Childhood sweethearts：指从小一起长大的异性朋友，常用来形容深厚的感情基础。
- 情书 (qíng shū) - Love Letter：表达爱意的书信。
- 岁月 (suì yuè) - Years：时间流逝的概念，常用来形容长久的情感积累。
- 守护 (shǒu hù) - Protect and Guard：默默地保护和支持。

英文版故事

At the edge of an ancient town stood an old wutong tree, which had witnessed countless seasons. Beneath its sprawling branches, a romantic tale unfolded across time—the story of Li Ming and Su Wan, childhood friends who grew up together, unaware of the budding love between them.

As the years flew by, Li Ming, each year on the first snowfall, secretly buried a handwritten love letter beneath the tree, chronicling his deepening affection for Su Wan. These letters, like messengers of time, patiently awaited their moment to be discovered. Meanwhile, Su Wan, though unaware of Li Ming's feelings, always sensed his warmth and companionship, nurturing her own feelings in secret.

A decade passed, and both had grown into adulthood, their lives carried away by the currents of time. Yet, on a winter afternoon, Su Wan stumbled upon the letters while sorting through old belongings. As she read each one, her heart overflowed with tears, realizing the silent devotion she had overlooked.

Determined, she penned her own reply, not just a response to the past but a promise for their future together. When Li Ming returned to the tree, he was stunned to find Su Wan's letter, and their emotions could no longer be contained. Under the very same wutong tree that had witnessed their growth, they embraced, vowing to spend the rest of their lives together.

Chapter 17: The Vow Beneath the Starlight

标题

- 中文：星光下的誓言
- 拼音：Xīng Guāng Xià De Shì Yán
- English: The Vow Beneath the Starlight

故事

在一个温柔的夏夜，小镇的边缘，有一片被古老传说笼罩的森林。李明（Lǐ Míng）与苏婉（Sū Wǎn），两位青梅竹马，相约在这片星光璀璨的林间空地。月光如洗，星星点点，仿佛是大自然最精致的布景，只为见证他们即将许下的誓言。

李明轻轻拉起苏婉的手，两人的目光在星光下交汇，充满了对未来的无限憧憬与坚定。"婉儿，记得小时候我们总爱数星星，说每一颗都藏着我们的梦想。"他温柔地说，"现在，我想告诉你，无论未来的路有多远多难，我都愿意成为你的星空，为你指引方向，守护你的每一个梦想。"

苏婉的眼眶微湿，笑容却比星光还要灿烂。"明哥哥，我也一直相信，我们的爱会像这些星星一样，虽然微小，却能穿越黑暗，照亮彼此的世界。我愿意与你携手，共赴每一个明天。"

于是，在这星光与月光的见证下，他们交换了最真挚的誓言，许下了相守一生的承诺。那一刻，时间仿佛静止，只留下两颗心紧紧相依，以及夜空中最亮的星光，为他们的爱情加冕。

关键词及含义

- 青梅竹马（qīng méi zhú mǎ）：childhood sweethearts
- 星光璀璨（xīng guāng cuǐ càn）：twinkling stars
- 誓言（shì yán）：vow, pledge
- 守护（shǒu hù）：protect, guard
- 梦想（mèng xiǎng）：dream
- 相爱相守（xiāng ài xiāng shǒu）：love and stay together

英文版故事

On a gentle summer night, at the edge of a small town, there lay a forest shrouded in ancient legends. Li Ming and Su Wan, two childhood sweethearts, met at a clearing beneath the starlit sky. The moonlight bathed everything in a silver glow, while the stars twinkled like nature's finest decorations, poised to bear witness to the vows they were about to make.

Li Ming gently took Su Wan's hand, their gazes meeting under the starlight, filled with visions of the future and unwavering determination. "Waner, remember when we used to count stars as children, saying each one held our dreams?" he said softly. "Now, I want to tell you that no matter how far or difficult the road ahead may be, I am willing to be your sky, guiding you and protecting every one of your dreams."

Su Wan's eyes glistened with tears, yet her smile shone brighter than the stars. "Ming Gege, I've always believed that our love, like these stars, though small, can traverse darkness and illuminate each other's worlds. I am willing to walk hand in hand with you, into every tomorrow."

And so, beneath the starlight and moonlight, they exchanged the most sincere vows, pledging their commitment to spend their lives together. In that moment, time seemed to stand still, leaving only two hearts intertwined and the brightest stars in the night sky, crowning their love.

Chapter 18: Eternal Kiss

标题：永恒之吻 - Yǒng Héng Zhī Wěn - Eternal Kiss

故事：

在古老而神秘的雾隐镇（Wù Yǐn Zhèn），有一个传说，每当七夕节（Qī Xī Jié）之夜，天空中最亮的两颗星会化作恋人，于银河之上留下一吻，这吻蕴含着无尽的爱意与承诺，被世人称为"永恒之吻"。

李明（Lǐ Míng），一位温文尔雅的年轻画家，自幼便对星空充满无限遐想。他相信每个星辰背后都有一段未了的故事，而他最大的愿望，就是能亲眼见证那传说中的永恒之吻。

同年，镇上搬来了一位名叫苏婉（Sū Wǎn）的女孩，她有着如银河般璀璨的双眸和温柔如水的性格。两人因一次偶然的机会在镇上的老槐树下相遇，从此，李明的生活里便多了一抹不同寻常的色彩。

随着时间的推移，他们共同度过了无数个日夜，从春日赏花到冬日观雪，从讨论星空的奥秘到分享彼此的梦想。李明发现，每当与苏婉在一起时，自己总能感受到前所未有的宁静与幸福，仿佛整个世界都为之静止。

终于，又一年的七夕将至，李明决定邀请苏婉一同前往山顶，那里是他认为最接近星空的地方。当夜幕降临，万籁俱寂，只见满天繁星闪烁，银河横跨天际，美得令人窒息。就在这时，一颗流星划破长空，紧接着，两颗异常明亮的星星缓缓靠近，仿佛真的在银河之上轻轻相吻。

李明转头看向苏婉，眼中满是深情："婉儿，我想我找到了我的永恒之吻，它不在星辰之间，而在这里，与你相守的每一刻。"说着，他缓缓靠近，给了苏婉一个温柔而坚定的吻。

那一刻，时间仿佛真的静止了，两颗心紧紧相连，成为了彼此生命中最美的风景。他们相信，只要心中有爱，每一个平凡的日子都能成为永恒。

关键词及英语含义：

- 雾隐镇（Wù Yǐn Zhèn）：Hidden Mist Town
- 七夕节（Qī Xī Jié）：Double Seventh Festival
- 永恒之吻（Yǒng Héng Zhī Wěn）：Eternal Kiss

- 李明（Lǐ Míng）：Li Ming
- 苏婉（Sū Wǎn）：Su Wan
- 银河（Yín Hé）：Milky Way
- 恋人（Liàn Rén）：Lovers
- 画家（Huà Jiā）：Painter
- 星空（Xīng Kōng）：Starry Sky
- 传说（Chuán Shuō）：Legend
- 承诺（Chéng Nuò）：Promise
- 温柔（Wēn Róu）：Gentle
- 宁静（Níng Jìng）：Serenity
- 流星（Liú Xīng）：Shooting Star
- 相守（Xiāng Shǒu）：Stay Together

英文版故事：

In the ancient and mystical town of Hidden Mist, there lies a legend that on the night of the Double Seventh Festival, the brightest stars in the sky transform into lovers, leaving behind an eternal kiss upon the Milky Way, imbued with boundless love and promise.

Li Ming, a gentle young painter, has always been fascinated by the stars and believed that each one holds an untold story. His greatest wish was to witness this legendary Eternal Kiss with his own eyes.

One year, a girl named Su Wan moved to the town, with eyes as sparkling as the galaxy and a gentle demeanor. Their paths crossed beneath an old locust tree, and from then on, Li Ming's life took on a new hue.

As time passed, they spent countless days and nights together, from admiring spring flowers to watching winter snowflakes, discussing the mysteries of the starry sky and sharing their dreams. Li Ming found that whenever he was with Su Wan, he felt an unprecedented peace and happiness, as if the entire world stood still.

Finally, the Double Seventh Festival arrived once again. Li Ming invited Su Wan to join him on the mountaintop, where he believed he could be closest to the stars. As night fell, silence enveloped everything, and the sky was filled with twinkling stars, the Milky Way stretching across the horizon in breathtaking beauty. Suddenly, a shooting star streaked across the sky, followed by two unusually bright stars slowly drawing closer, as if truly kissing above the galaxy.

Turning to Su Wan, Li Ming's eyes brimming with affection, he said, "Wan'er, I think I've found my Eternal Kiss. It's not among the stars, but here, in every moment spent with you." With that, he gently and firmly pressed his lips to hers.

In that instant, time

Chapter 19: A Heartwarming Romance Story

标题

温馨的浪漫故事
Wēn Xīn De Làng Màn Gù Shì
A Heartwarming Romance Story

故事

在一个被夕阳染成橘红色的傍晚，李明（Lǐ Míng）与苏婉（Sū Wǎn）漫步在小镇的老街上。街道两旁，古老的梧桐树轻轻摇曳，仿佛在低语着过往的情愫。李明突然停下脚步，从口袋里掏出一枚精致的银戒指，上面刻着两人的名字缩写，在夕阳的余晖下闪闪发光。

"婉儿，从我们相遇的那一刻起，我的世界就变得不同了。"李明深情地望着苏婉，眼中闪烁着温柔的光芒，"我想用这枚戒指，锁住我们未来的每一个瞬间，你愿意吗？"

苏婉的眼眶微湿，她紧紧握住李明的手，仿佛害怕这一切只是梦境。"明，我愿意，与你携手共度每一个晨曦与黄昏。"她的声音虽轻，却充满了坚定与幸福。

两人相视一笑，周围的世界仿佛都为之静止。在那一刻，时间不再是匆匆过客，而是成为了他们爱情最温柔的见证者。

关键词及含义

- **温馨**（Wēn Xīn）：warm and tender
- **浪漫**（Làng Màn）：romantic
- **夕阳**（Xī Yáng）：sunset
- **老街**（Lǎo Jiē）：old street
- **梧桐树**（Wú Tóng Shù）：plane tree
- **银戒指**（Yín Jiè Zhi）：silver ring
- **情愫**（Qíng Sù）：feelings
- **晨曦**（Chén Xī）：dawn
- **黄昏**（Huáng Hūn）：dusk
- **携手**（Xié Shǒu）：hold hands together

英文版故事

On an evening tinted orange by the setting sun, Li Ming and Su Wan strolled down the old street of the small town. Alongside, ancient plane trees swayed gently, whispering tales of bygone affections. Suddenly, Li Ming halted, reaching into his pocket to pull out a delicate silver ring, engraved with their initials, gleaming under the afterglow of the sunset.

"Wan'er, since the moment we met, my world has never been the same," Li Ming gazed at Su Wan with profound affection, his eyes twinkling with tenderness. "I want to use this ring to seal every moment of our future. Will you?"

Su Wan's eyes moistened as she clasped Li Ming's hand tightly, as if afraid this was all but a dream. "Ming, I do, I want to walk through every dawn and dusk with you," she said softly, her voice filled with resolve and happiness.

They smiled at each other, and the world around them seemed to stand still. In that instant, time ceased to be a fleeting visitor, but rather, the gentlest witness to their love.

Chapter 20: Love that Captivates a City

标题

倾城之恋 (Qīng Chéng Zhī Liàn) - Love that Captivates a City

故事

在古老的江南水乡，有一座被岁月温柔以待的小镇，名唤云隐（Yún Yǐn）。这里，春日里桃花笑春风，夏日荷叶连天碧，秋来枫叶染红霜，冬至雪覆青瓦白墙。就在这如诗如画的景致中，发生了一段倾城之恋。

男主角陆辰（Lù Chén），一位温文尔雅的年轻画师，常于河畔柳下，以笔为媒，绘尽人间烟火。女主角苏婉（Sū Wǎn），则是镇上出了名的才女，琴棋书画样样精通，更有一副清丽脱俗的容颜，仿佛从画中走出。

一次偶然的机会，陆辰在镇上的桃花林中偶遇了苏婉，她正轻抚古琴，一曲《高山流水》悠扬而出，引得四周花瓣轻舞。那一刻，时间仿佛静止，陆辰的心被深深触动，他知道，这便是他一直在寻找的灵感之源，也是命中注定的缘分。

自那以后，陆辰便常借故探访苏婉，两人从诗词歌赋谈到人生理想，渐生情愫。他们一起漫步于古镇的青石板路上，共赏夕阳下的波光粼粼，月下花前，许下了相守一生的誓言。

然而，好景不长，一场突如其来的战乱打破了小镇的宁静。为了保护苏婉，陆辰决定参军入伍，临行前夜，两人在镇口的老槐树下紧紧相拥，泪水与月光交织成一幅动人心魄的画面。

几年后，战争结束，陆辰带着满身的伤痕与荣耀归来，却发现云隐镇已物是人非。但幸运的是，在熟悉的小巷深处，他再次见到了那个让他魂牵梦绕的身影——苏婉，她依旧美丽，只是眼中多了几分坚韧与等待。

两人重逢，没有过多的言语，只有紧紧相拥，泪水与欢笑交织成世间最美的风景。从此，他们在云隐镇重建家园，陆辰的画中多了一位永恒的女主角，而他们的故事，也成为了镇上流传千古的佳话，倾动了整个城市的心。

关键词及英语含义

- **云隐 (Yún Yǐn)**: Hidden Cloud Village (a poetic name for the town)
- **陆辰 (Lù Chén)**: Lu Chen (male protagonist)

- 苏婉 **(Sū Wǎn)**: Su Wan (female protagonist)
- 倾城之恋 **(Qīng Chéng Zhī Liàn)**: Love that Captivates a City (a romantic story that moves the entire city)
- 桃花林 **(Táo Huā Lín)**: Peach Blossom Forest (a picturesque setting)
- 战乱 **(Zhàn Luàn)**: War and Chaos (a period of conflict)
- 重逢 **(Chóng Féng)**: Reunion (meeting again after a long separation)

英文版故事

In the ancient waterside town of Yunyin, nestled amidst the serene landscapes of southern China, a romance unfolded that captivated the hearts of all. This was the tale of Lu Chen, a gentle young painter, and Su Wan, the town's renowned beauty and scholar.

Lu Chen often found solace by the riverbank, his brushstrokes capturing the essence of daily life. Su Wan, with her exquisite features and mastery of music, poetry, calligraphy, and painting, seemed to have stepped out of one of Lu Chen's own paintings.

Fate brought them together in a blossoming peach grove, where Su Wan's melodious tune on the guqin entranced Lu Chen. From that moment on, their conversations ranged from poetry to dreams, fostering a bond that transcended time.

But war descended upon the peaceful town, shattering its tranquility. Lu Chen enlisted to protect Su Wan, promising to return. Their parting beneath the old locust tree was a poignant scene, etched in the hearts of all who witnessed it.

Years later, Lu Chen returned scarred but victorious, only to find Yunyin forever changed. Yet, in the depths of a familiar alleyway, he found Su Wan, still as beautiful, but now with a strength forged by waiting.

Their reunion was a silent embrace, tears mingling with laughter. Together, they rebuilt their lives in Yunyin, Lu Chen's canvases forever adorned with the image of his beloved. Their story became a legend, a love that captivated not just the town but the hearts of all who heard it, forever etched in the annals of time.

Milton Keynes UK
Ingram Content Group UK Ltd.
UKHW011015290724
446271UK00012B/491